Rascals

Weird, Wacky, and Wonderful Stories from an Inner-City Church

ROB LINK

©2012 Reformed Church Press

Dedication

I wrote this book for all the wonderful rascals at The River. It is a privilege to call The River my church home. Thank you for letting me share our story. I love you all and count it an honor to be one of your pastors.

Other books by Rob Link

Pulse: You Can't Heal What You Can't Feel

The King of Rascals

Introduction

Rascal, n.: *Someone who behaves in a mischievous way, whether intentionally or not.*

September 2004. That's when it all began. The wonderful craziness. I suppose, at least in part, it was my own fault.

A year earlier I had started to get this yearning in my gut to start a church. A church where anyone and everyone would be welcomed and embraced so that they might encounter Jesus.

I had been in full-time vocational ministry for a number of years and had yet to see a church where the homeless and the homemaker could worship side by side. Where those without a penny could sing unto the Lord next to those with plenty. Where the addicted, burnt out, tattered, torn, tired, unkempt poor could encounter Jesus while sitting next to the addicted, burnt out, tattered, torn, tired, unkempt wealthy.

So the wonderful craziness that kicked off in 2004 was partly my fault. But to be fully forthcoming, most of the blame rests on God. It was really his idea to create a new Christ-following community that all folks—especially the underprivileged—could call home. It was God's passion to see the haves and the have-nots come together as the body of Christ. It was his idea to start something new and a little different (maybe a lot different for Kalamazoo, Michigan). It was God who put those yearnings in my gut. I was simply following orders.

Those gut-urgings came to fruition that Sunday in September 2004.

A ministry called The River was born.

And the craziness began. The wonderful craziness.

This book is a collection of stories and encounters that we have had over the years here at The River. Some are funny, so feel free to laugh. Some are tragic, so feel free to cry. Some are confusing, so feel free to scratch your head.

I tell these stories with two audiences in mind. First, they are for all the church planters out there serving with blood, sweat, and tears in an effort to reach people who do not yet know God's awesome love for them. It is tough work. It is often discouraging work. Yet from time to time there are moments of Holy Spirit magic: someone who once was blind receives sight; someone who once was lost gets found. I'm writing for you church planters to encourage you to keep on going. The kingdom of God needs you.

Second, I'm writing for my friends at The River who lived through these experiences with me. To you I say, remember, it is for such wonderful, crazy people as these that Jesus came. Remember, it is for scallywags and scoundrels like these that we exist as a church. Remember how boring life would be out in the suburbs. I'm glad we can remember together.

Oh, and by the way, most names have been changed, as have a detail or two from time to time, because that's what you do in a book like this. And I'm recording the events as best my memory serves.

One more thing before we get rolling.

You might be asking yourself, "Rascals? Why did Rob title this book *Rascals*?"

If you are asking, I'll tell you why. If you aren't, I'll tell you anyway.

In my book *King of Rascals*, I answered the question, How much does the King of kings love sinful people, i.e. rascals, like us?

Answer: A ton.

Throughout the Bible we read story after story of Jesus sticking up for and fighting for the underdog, the sinner, the rascal. Amazing.

The King of kings loves rascals. A ton.

In this book we focus on the ones Jesus loves—the rascals.

Thus the title: *Rascals.*

Enjoy it, you rascal!

Oh, and one more thing. I mean it this time. Just one more thing. All artwork is done by my son Jake and me. His doodles are the better ones.

1
Tom, Betty, and Ted

They called him Big Sexy. If there ever was an oxymoron, that was it.

He had to weigh over 350 pounds. Tom lived right next door to our first building over on Lake Street. His favorite pastime was sitting on his porch and shouting hello to the world as it passed him by. And he rarely did it with a shirt on. Big Sexy.

His rotund belly would jiggle as he laughed in a way that would make Santa jealous.

Where I come from, folks have this thing they call modesty. Big Sexy had no idea what that word meant.

It wasn't long before he became a regular at The River. We quickly discovered that he was mildly mentally impaired and lived with his wife who was also mentally impaired. Her name was Betty. They lived with Ted, who was also mildly impaired.

Turns out Betty used to be Tom's babysitter when he was a little kid. She was married to Ted at the time she was Tom's baby sitter. But by the time I met them, Tom and Betty were married and Ted was living in their house as a renter. Betty had fallen for little Tommy, and when he came of age Ted was left in the lurch and she married Tom. Talk about an interesting love triangle. It was the stuff Jerry Springer made a living on.

And yet these three gentle spirits made it work. There wasn't a lick of animosity between them. Ted didn't seem slighted in the least bit.

It probably helped that Ted was a prolific dater. About once a month he would show up in my office with a new woman in tow and ask if I would marry them. As kindly as I could, I declined each invitation to marry Ted to some poor woman. Didn't faze Ted a bit. He kept right on dating and asking me to perform his wedding.

2
Fido

Fido got baptized. At The River. During a Sunday service.

My goodness, please do not tell my theology profs. They would have a heart attack.

I had overheard one of our elders say, "I'm sorry, we don't baptize dogs." Not every day you hear that phrase, is it?

It was a baptism day at The River. Our elders were working hard collecting contact information, checking to see if the person who wanted to be baptized was plugged into a group, and most importantly if the person knew all about Jesus. At The River, it isn't uncommon for an elder to gently direct an individual back to his or her seat. Usually a guy who had been baptized a hundred times over the years and wanted another go, or a mother who was visiting, had no connection to the church, and wanted her newborn baby baptized. But I had never heard, "Sorry, we don't baptize dogs."

Ellen had been a part of The River for some time. She was as normal as you and me (whatever normal is), except for one thing. She carried this little, mangy dog in a baby sling attached to her front. Never saw her without Fido. Ellen and Fido. Fido and Ellen. They were like some freaky version of conjoined twins.

She took the news fairly well that we weren't going to baptize Fido and decided to continue with her own baptism. She was a newer believer and figured it was time to get baptized with or without Fido. So as she leaned over the baptismal font, as the elder at hand doused her with some good old H_2O, Fido was not to be denied. Fido strained with all the might her little body had, reached as far away from the baby sling as she could, and made a watery mess as she vigorously slapped at the bowl holding the water. Both Ellen and Fido came away soaking wet.

My kids, who happened to be in the front row, came away with sore bellies from laughing so hard.

In the end, Fido got baptized. At The River. During a Sunday service.

3
Richard

The first time I met him I said, "Hey, I'm Rob. What's your name?"

"Names are just social constructs our parents label us with to control us and box us in with."

Hmmm... okaaay. "Well, whatever you go by, it's good to be standing here with you on this spot."

"All ground is an illusion. This spot we are standing on isn't really here. It is simply part of the cosmos and a greater reality that we can never comprehend."

Thus began a several-year friendship between The River and Richard.

Unlike Tom, Betty, and Ted, Richard was not mentally impaired. He was just weird. It's actually really rather sad. He used this pseudo-intellect stuff to keep people at arm's length. It was his defense mechanism to protect himself from getting hurt. He had been hurt many times.

I remember one Sunday during the service our prayer team was ministering to people. Richard came forward for prayer. He launched into another confused diatribe about reality and our perception (or lack thereof) of it. The guy praying for Richard gently said something along the lines of: "I think you hide behind all that baloney. What's going on at a deeper level?"

Oh my. You would have thought someone had spit in his face or desecrated his mother's grave.

In 0.3 seconds flat, Richard went from calm, passive, peace loving, quasi-hippy to Genghis Khan. He slammed the elder against the wall and commenced a verbal tirade liberally laced with the f-bomb.

After the wall slam, Richard regained control. Turned and walked out. End of story.

I guess our prayer person touched a nerve.

4
Walt

"He must've been sleepy," I said to myself the first time Walt fell asleep during our midweek prayer service.

Walt was a lonely guy who found a home at The River. He came, was loved, made friends, would go on retreats, and encountered the risen King.

And he would fall asleep every time he came to a service. And he would snore. Loudly. Each Thursday night. It was part of our weekly routine. Fraaz would lead worship, I'd teach, and Walt would snore.

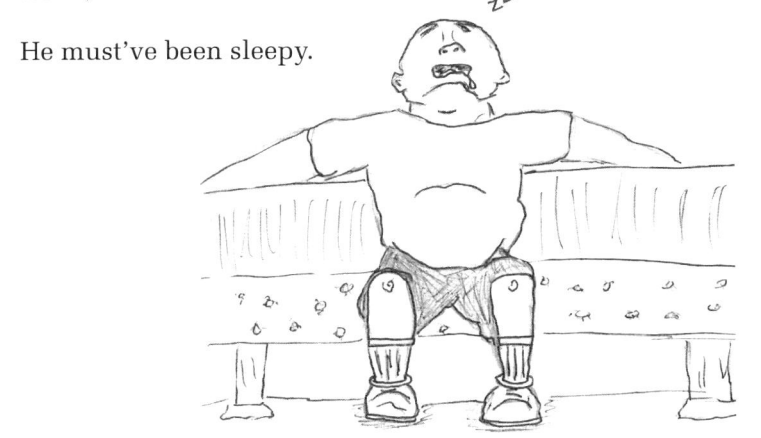

He must've been sleepy.

5
Baby Mama

One day all the kids in our nursery learned how to swear like a sailor.

She was the mama of his baby. He was an idiot. They had a falling out soon after the kid was born. She had custody. He didn't.

Unbeknowst to her he had shown up at The River that day. After the service he quickly made his way to the nursery in an effort to take their child before she got there. Fortunately our care providers are trained to handle such monkey business. He was getting nowhere with our volunteers when she walked in. She quickly deduced what he was trying to do.

That's when all hades broke loose. She unleashed a verbal onslaught that contained every four letter word known to humanity. I think she even invented a few new ones. And she was loud. Very loud.

Everyone within a mile radius watched the air turn blue. And the kids learned a lot of new words.

6
Sexism (Kinda)

Our first building was really old and sort of run down. Not only did it house us, The River, it housed mice. Lots and lots of mice. It wasn't uncommon to be seated, talking to some folks, and they would stop making eye contact and stare with horror over your shoulder at the mouse perched on the rail. Yuck. I think we single-handedly kept the local exterminators in the black.

I remember one time our kids built these awesome paper-maché trees. They were really cool. I found them artistic. The mice found them tasty. We'd be seated in a circle trying to do some kind of business, and all we could concentrate on was the multitude of little mice feet we heard scurrying around inside those trees. Ick.

I'm not ashamed to say that I hate mice. Can't stand them. They give me the heebie jeebies. I know it's irrational, but I can't help it. I can't stand mice. Whenever I see one, dead or alive, I just get the shivers. Just thinking about them as I type this makes me squirm.

I mentioned the local exterminators. They taught me something. The mouse poison they placed in various and sundry places all around the church was nothing more than mouse-lethal-doses of Coumadin. You might not know that Coumadin is a drug used as a blood thinner often prescribed to people who've had blood clots. The little monstrosities at our church would nibble on it, try to squeeze through a tight space, and bleed to death internally. Nasty business. Just plain ol' nasty.

Do you know that story in the book of Ezekiel where the prophet is led through the valley of dry bones? At times we would walk into the basement and it would feel like we were walking into Ezekiel's vision—only on a mousie scale. There were dead mice everywhere. It looked like a rodent armegeddon (that might be a bit of an exaggeration—but I'm making a point here!). If Fraaz was around he would heroically dispose of the tiny corpses. Not only can he lead a large gathering of people to the throne of God as our worship pastor, he's also not afraid of mice. Very useful guy to have around.

Yet when it was just me, our children's pastor, and our administrative assistant in the building, the job fell to me. And for just one reason. They are women and I'm a man. Some moron once told these two otherwise savvy women that dead-mice-removal is a man's job. Nothing I said could convince them otherwise. I was stuck. One morning I walked in and saw a mouse had died underneath the drippy drinking fountain. Not only did I have to remove a dead mouse, I had to remove a soggy dead mouse. Gross.

Can't tell you how many times I about barfed carrying out dead mice. Just because I'm male.

Not fair.

Sexism. Kinda.

7
Two Bucks

Not long after we started The River, we had outgrown our building on Lake St. We needed a much larger sanctuary. One that held 500 people would be nice. But providing services for multiple homeless folks and college students translated into a very tight budget. On our way home from a conference, four of us prayed that the Lord would give us a building. We figured the Bible says you have not because you ask not, so we'd ask for a building. One that was much larger. One that was free.

Guess what? Prayer is powerful and effective. The Southwest Michigan Classis of the Reformed Church in America called. They had a building and wondered if we would like it. I knew the building. It was huge. It was old and historical. And it was right smack dab in the middle of downtown Kalamazoo—the hub of the city where people of all socioeconomic statuses hang out. It would be perfect.

"Of course we'd like it," I said, "but we can't afford it." There was a slight chuckle on the other end of the line. "No, it's not for sale. We want to give it to you. For free." Amazing!

We learned that the paperwork would be much easier if we bought it. It would take four signatures for a purchase, and what seemed like a million signatures if it was gifted to us. So we agreed with the classis on the asking price of $2. Two dollars! For a building with land easily worth more than a million.

On the day I was to meet with the lawyers, our elder, and a classis representative, I realized I had no cash on me. Fortunately my mom was visiting. She floated me $2 so I could go buy a building. Thanks, Mom.

8
Sad Suits and Happy T-shirts

He'd never been to The River before. He only knew that we were somewhere downtown. The problem was that there are many churches downtown. He didn't know where to begin to find The River.

He told me he saw many folks coming out of downtown churches wearing suits and looking grumpy and sad. Then he saw a bunch of people coming out of this one church wearing T-shirts and they all looked happy.

He had found The River.

Sad suits and happy T-shirts.

9
"I ain't crazy…"

It's not uncommon for us to need assistance from the Kalamazoo Department of Public Safety, i.e., the cops. On this occasion there was this fella who was incredibly belligerent with our female staff members. And he was a big man. Needless to say, the women were nervous when he refused to leave the building. So they called the cops.

The officer on duty showed up right as Wil, Fraaz, and I did. She was all of 5'4". She couldn't have weighed more than 120 pounds soaking wet. The man she had been asked to remove was at least 6'2" and weighed well over two hundred pounds. It looked like things could get interesting.

The officer politely asked the guy to leave. He rolled his eyes. That was the wrong move.

Have you ever seen a cat puff up to twice its size? I swear to you this is exactly what happened with this policewoman! She put her index finger in his face and said, "Don't you roll your eyes at me. I ain't crazy. You are crazy. You are going to leave right now and not come back or you will take a ride in my car!" Each word punctuated with her extended index finger.

He left.

They say it isn't the size of the dog in the fight, it's the size of the fight in the dog. Must be true. That, or her gun scared him.

10
Puppy Love

We really like dogs at The River. So much so we have two on staff. Timber is Wil's dog and is in charge of connections on Sundays. After each service we invite new folks to have a treat with Timber in the "Treats with Timber" room. While with Timber they can ask any question in the world, learn about The River, and meet our executive pastor, Wil. As you know, going to a new church can be a bit scary. That fear is tripled by the thought of meeting with a pastor. Timber does wonders to set people at ease and make them feel comfortable. She does her job very well.

Barkly is my dog. He's a big old Newfoundland. Barkly works in the hospitality ministry as a greeter. Each Sunday, rain or shine, he and I stand outside and greet all the folks coming to church. It's remarkable how the walls come down instantly around this four-legged wonder. Kids love him. Adults love him. Everybody loves him.

I've seen the toughest people get down on the ground and let him lick all over their face. I've seen the most wounded, abused, and guarded individuals openly and warmly let him love on them. I've seen shy and nervous kids giggle like crazy when he shakes their hand. Like Timber, Barkly does his job very well.

Oh, and I forgot to mention, Timber and Barkly are dating.

11
Travel Mug

Every single Sunday, for months on end, he spilled his coffee on my dog's head.

And then he would say, "S#@!" Every Sunday. Without fail.

After the first time he swore, he apologized. It became a running joke in our family. We'd get home from church and have to brush dried coffee out of the dog's hair.

Then the next Sunday, my boys would stand back and watch as the guy approached the pooch, bent over to pet him, spilled his coffee, then swore. Every Sunday. They laughed each time. Every Sunday. Without fail.

For Christmas the Link family got him a travel mug.

12
More Coffee

There are times as a preacher when you know the people are right there with you. They are hanging on every word. You know that as you wind up the sermon they will be smacked wonderfully between the eyes with the point. You know there will be conviction, weeping, confession, and joy.

I remember one such day at The River. (I hope there has been more than one.) Folks were right there. The teaching was about to become a watershed moment in the lives of hundreds. I was about to deliver the final punch when…

"Aaaaarghhhh!"

Our building has a balcony. I remember as a kid loving to sit high above, looking down on the world. Turns out the balcony is still a favorite haunt of children today.

It happened just as I was about to deliver the sermon's knock-out punch. A little kid, in his normal, little-kid squirminess, knocked his mom's scalding hot coffee off the balcony rail right onto this dude sitting beneath them.

As I look back on that day, I have no idea what I preached on. No one does.

I asked.

13
Even More Coffee

Different day. Same thing. Different target.

This time an adult knocked his coffee off the balcony rail. Right smack dab into our sound booth. Yikes.

Fortunately it just landed on Cindy, who was running the computer that day. Better her than the computer.

Just don't tell her I said that.

14
Skid Marks

Murder was almost committed at our annual men's retreat.

Walt (who stars in Story 4 about snoring in church) thought it would be funny to play a joke on Chris.

Before we go any further, I need to let you know that Walt is mildly impaired. I would like to blame the following on that impairment.

Late one night, while Chris was in the camp kitchen preparing for the next morning's breakfast, Walt, with the full knowledge of the other eight men sharing the room, unleashed his little prank.

When Chris got back to the room it was dark. He quietly went about his business preparing for bed. He slipped into bed, eager to rest his weary bones.

As he placed his head on his pillow he felt a rough flakiness.

Then his nose caught a whiff of poop.

Walt had thought it would be funny to put his underwear

(rather large underwear I might add) over Chris's pillow. Unfortunately for Chris, Walt was less than thorough when it came to the paperwork after he would do his duty.

Thus the rough flaky feel.

Thus the poopy smell.

Thus Chris about murdered Walt.

15
Symbols and Signs

The Bible is filled with countless signs and symbols. This thing represents a bigger thing. That thing points to another thing. Water symbolizes new birth. Fire represents the powerful presence of the Almighty. A bird stands for the ever-present presence of the Counselor—the Holy Spirit.

One early morning, on my way into the building, I saw a powerful sign. Right there on the steps of the church was this massive bird. It had a wingspan of several feet. I instantly thought of Jesus' baptism, when a dove descended on him and he heard the voice of the Father.

I felt the urge, like Moses so long ago, to take off my shoes. Surely this was holy ground. I tilted my head to hear the Father better. And then… And then…

And then I saw that it was just a dead falcon.

Bummer.

16
Female Dog

Many times in my life as a church planter I have thought, hmmm… they didn't teach me about that in seminary.

Once while I was teaching this very un-sober man stood up and started talking very loudly. It was a bit distracting. As I mentioned earlier, Fraaz is a handy guy to have around. He quickly stood and approached the man. He put his arm around him to steer him toward the door.

This inebriated gentleman took exception to having Fraaz put his arm around his shoulder. At the top of his lungs he yelled, "I ain't your B#@!*, get off me!" Which was even more distracting.

I have no idea what I preached on that day. No one does.

I asked.

17
The Oldest Profession

I'm not kidding when I say his name was "Champagne." He was self-employed. As a male prostitute.

Business must have been slow, because he came to The River looking for a bus token. Thank goodness I was out of town that day. Wil answered the door.

When Champagne asked for a token, Wil said we were all out. So he asked for money. Wil said, "No, sir."

Up to this point in the story nothing all that unusual has taken place. If that were the end of the encounter, this little vignette would not have made this book. Here's why it did.

In exchange for some money Champagne offered Wil his professional services. Said he would change Wil's orientation.

You know what Wil was thinking?

Hmmm… they didn't teach about this in seminary.

18
Depends

We are incredibly proud (in a good way) that we have a ton of broken, messed up, weird people who call The River their home. People who have never in their life felt loved and accepted by a church are now part of a family known as The River.

We are very glad these folks call The River home. (And if you want to know the truth, broken, messed up, and weird describes all of us!)

Yet some of them bring unique challenges to us that we are ill-prepared to deal with.

Like William. He is in his mid-50s. William comes to church with a few folks that he lives with in a group home. He is incredibly gentle-spirited. He is kind, soft-spoken, tender-hearted. Both The River and my life are enriched because he is in it.

His unique challenge? Incontinence. Poor fella can't hold his bladder. It's very embarrassing for him. On more than one occasion he has wet his pants and the chair right in the middle of the service.

He loves to sit in the front row, so when he jumps up with wet pants from a soggy chair in the middle of the teaching or in the midst of a baptism, it's hard not to notice.

A few of the men minister to him with great love and care and dignity. When he has an accident a couple of guys help him out of the sanctuary as discreetly as possible. They take him to the men's room, grab some extra pants they have stashed for just this moment, and help him get cleaned and changed.

While that is going on, another man quietly pulls the chair off to the side and turns it over so no one will sit on it until it's cleaned later in the week. Then these guys help William back to the front row and sit with an arm around his shoulder to let him know everything is ok.

That's beautiful.

19
A Crappy Idea

Our building is located smack-dab in the middle of Kalamazoo. Among other things it is the hub for the city's homeless population. As you might imagine, homeless people need to use the bathroom too. It wasn't unusual for us to arrive in the morning to discover…ah…how shall we say it…evidence that some folks had attended to the necessary.

So we thought it would be a good idea to rent a port-a-potty, place it discreetly on our property, and let our homeless brothers or sisters have some dignity when those late night urges arose.

The third morning we had the port-a-potty, we found that it had been tipped over, giving us both olfactory and visual evidence it had been put to good use the prior two days.

Not easily daunted in our good deed, we called the rental company. They came with haz-mat suits, cleaned it up, set it up, and we were ready to roll.

Two nights later, same thing. So we called the rental company...

Four nights later, same thing. Grrrrrr. Now it was personal. We needed to come up with a plan. One that would solve our problem. The prankster(s) had to be stopped, and our friends had to have access to a bathroom in the middle of the night.

Staff at The River have a lot of education floating around. Several college degrees. A number of master's degrees. Shoot, we even have two master of divinity degrees at our church. Up against that mind-power, the pranksters were sure to be thwarted. There was no way they would be able to overcome our collective brilliance in devising a plan to make the can tip-proof.

We gave hours (or maybe two minutes) of thought to how we could solve this problem. Plans were laid. Action was taken. Orders were executed. Port-a-potty was staked to the ground with stakes long enough to make a vampire nervous. It was brilliant. A marvel of engineering.

It was tipped over that very night.

We don't have a port-a-potty any more.

20.22

Charlie was a regular. He also was an alcoholic. But, as they say, he was a "friendly drunk."

One evening, at prayer service, he came in a little drunker than usual. The norm was for him to come in, sit down, and rest peacefully as we prayed. On this particular evening the norm fell by the wayside.

He ambled down the aisle not really caring if we were in the midst of a service and began loudly declaring that he had wet his pants. A brief inspection proved that, sure enough, he had wet his pants.

Turns out he was having problems with his prostate. He was Hispanic and had little mastery over the English language. So he loudly began to declare his problems with his, umm…private areas.

He used "modern American idioms" to describe his private areas, meaning he used words that would make grandma roll over in her grave. He did this in church. With a bunch of kids present. (I see a theme here at The River. Hmmm…)

Here is what made the encounter even more interesting. In his broken English he went on to describe how he had felt unsafe sleeping out in the park at night. It took him a while to get his point across. In fact he had a very hard time getting his point across until...

Well, until he pulled out a gun—a loaded gun—and began to wave it around, showing it to the people. He seemed to be trying to communicate that this was how he kept himself safe. Folks at the prayer meeting might have understood him to be asking for prayers for his protection, because the moment he brought the gun out the prayer-level rose considerably.

After he had waved the gun in my face for the tenth time (just showing me, of course, he really didn't mean to be threatening), it dawned on me this might not be safe. I remembered when I was a kid I had seen *The Karate Kid*—remember that movie? I harkened back to how Daniel learned to "wax off" as a way of martial-arts-ly protecting himself. So as Charlie waved his gun in the air, I "waxed off" in a way that would have made Mr. Miyagi proud. The gun went flying. I was the hero.

Okay, only in my imagination. I really just asked him to put his gun away, and he did.

But the karate-kid thing sounds a lot cooler.

21
Good Help

We had made a bad hire or two in our history. Not the right chemistry. Character issues. You know. That kinda stuff.

When Wil transitioned from site pastor into the role of executive pastor, he made it clear that he wanted to do the hiring. "It will cut down on those bad-hire headaches," he said. Actually, he didn't just say that, he promised that.

We needed a new administrative assistant. Wil put an all-points bulletin out to all the places you advertise such things. He scoured through thousands—maybe millions—of applications. He conducted countless interviews. After many hours of scouring, praying, fasting, and blood, sweat, and tears, he hired Dorothy. She was the one for us. Without question!

Her first day was January 11, 2010. Started at 9:00 a.m.

Her last day was January 11, 2010. Quit at noon.

Never came back. Worked one half-day. That was it.

Having an executive pastor sure has saved me a lot of headaches.

22
A Sad One

So far most of the stories have been funny or touching. Here's a really sad one.

When he came to my office one afternoon, Paul had just gotten out of jail. Our meeting was the beginning of an eighteen-month friendship. Not just with me, but with numbers of folks at The River. Paul became a semi-regular presence in my home. We did Easter and Christmas together. He played with my kids. Jake still has fond memories of him.

He hadn't been a violent criminal. He had been nabbed for impersonating a doctor, forging checks, and a few other schemes. He had had a very messed up, abusive past. Throughout his whole life he had struggled with questions of worth and significance. He wondered if anyone loved him. He wondered if he had any value. Heavy depression was his constant companion. Out of all this he made some dumb choices. He was simply trying to make ends meet the way he knew how.

Back to our first meeting. After talking, and sharing how lonely he was, he decided to become a Christ-follower right there in my office. It was the real thing. As the days, weeks, and months passed he grew in his walk with the Lord. His probation officer told me on more than one occasion that she wished more of her cases were like Paul's. He was truly changing. Not only had Paul met Jesus, he had found a home and friends who really loved him. And he knew his new friends loved him.

But then his past caught up with him. Folks that he had done shady business with before his incarceration came calling for his services again. (He was good with a computer and could forge certain things that were tough to forge.) He said, "No thanks, I'm done with that."

They threatened to call his probation officer and tell her about all the other illegal things he had done that the authorities didn't yet know about. I believe it's called blackmail.

Paul went back into business. It wasn't long though before his newfound conscience kicked in. He knew what he was doing was wrong. Not just illegal, but wrong. He was a Christ-follower and wanted to do what was right. He told his associates just that. They threatened again. Not just with blackmail, but with violence this time.

So he ran. Left the city. Left the county. Left the state. He ran away.

He failed to check in with his probation officer. A warrant was filed for his arrest.

Occasionally he would call me to "check in." On one of his calls he told me that he was in a psychiatric hospital in Chicago. He had swallowed a whole bottle of Tylenol in an effort to end his life. He wanted me to come visit, but he didn't want me to tell the police.

I called a lawyer friend, who told me that I didn't have to call the police as I was his pastor. I don't know if that was true, but I believed him at the time.

Paul told me where to find him and the alias he had checked into the hospital under. When I saw him, he was broken. I became broken too. We cried. A lot.

Before I left him, we had arranged for me to pick him up when he was discharged, take him back to Kalamazoo, and walk him through the necessary steps to make things right with the law.

We talked a couple more times, arranging the details. Then late one night his grandma called my house. I had never in my life talked to her. I was sorta shocked when she introduced herself.

I was even more shocked when she told me her grandson,

my friend, had hung himself that night with the sheets from his hospital bed.

23
Another Sad One

Albert helped us start The River several years ago. He was a wealthy Englishman employed as an engineer. He and his wife, Valerie, added a ton to our launch team. They not only love God and are very gifted, they have cool accents.

We knew he had struggled with alcohol in the past, but we had no idea how big those struggles were.

Once when I was at a men's conference, preparing to speak, I saw Albert come through the door and make his way toward me. My first thought was, "Awesome. It's good to see a familiar face in a room full of strangers."

Yet as he drew closer it became apparent that all was not well. To begin with he staggered on wobbly legs. When he was still ten feet away I could smell the overwhelming odor of alcohol. The guy wasn't a little tipsy. He was absolutely drunk.

Albert wasn't a mean alcoholic. Nor was he a loud one. He was a morose alcoholic. When he drank (which we discovered was most of the time) he became very sad.

Moments before I was to go on stage to speak to a room full of men, he latched onto me and started to bawl. My shirt got soaked with tears and snot. A couple men who were hosting the event gently led Albert to a side room to minister to him as I walked on the stage to preach.

That was the last I saw of him for over two years.

I was speaking at the local gospel mission, and guess who I saw seated in the front row of homeless men. Albert.

His addiction had kicked his butt. He had gone from affluent owner of a home on a lake and happily married, to homeless divorced person.

Although it was a sad place to find him, our reunion was wonderful. It was really good to see him again.

He started coming to The River. He got plugged in with one of our men's groups. He had found a family and love again. He was our friend. He knew he was loved. It really looked like he was walking in victory, and that this was a great, praise-God, success story.

This lasted for a few years.

Then he disappeared again.

Wil got a call from Albert's ex-wife. She shared some

really awful news.

Albert had taken some money from the recent sale of their home, paid several weeks in advance at a long-stay hotel, and commenced to drink himself to death. By the time the manager went to check on the room once the prepay had run out, Albert was dead, his blood fatally thinned by enormous amounts of alcohol.

They had to use dental records to identify his body.

24
Peace

The last two stories were rough to write. Two of our friends were so beaten in this life that ending life was the route they took. I hate that. I miss those guys.

There is a thought that does bring me a lot of comfort in the midst of the yuckiness.

These two fellas really loved Jesus. Jesus tells us that we are saved by grace through faith and not as a result of our works. The apostle Paul says that anyone who calls on the name of the Lord will be saved.

Ahhh... Our two friends were saved by grace. Their suffering is over. For them pain is no more.

For them, peace. At last.

25
Timmmberrrrr

Bob was big. Real big. We're talking 6'8", 350 pounds. That's big.

Not only was he big, he had epilepsy. And seizures.

I'm not sure if you know what happens to someone who has a seizure. The person loses much of their muscle control and often falls over.

This is what would happen to Bob. He would fall over. And there was a lot of him to fall.

I recall one time as he was seizing while seated, he fell over toward a small woman seated next to him. She leapt to safety, barely escaping injury as he came crashing down right where she had been seated.

Another time Bob was standing when a seizure hit him. It took four relatively big men to catch him and save the children who were standing right in front of him from harm.

At one of our prayer/healing services, Bob asked if we could pray for his epilepsy to be removed. We did.

It was. Praise God! No more seizures.

And the church had become a safer place to be.

26
One More about Bob

Bob loved to dance. One Easter we had assembled a dance team to promenade down the aisle. There were several mothers, a number of female college students, a couple of high school girls, and Bob. All 6'8", 350 pounds of him.

It was an awesome sight to behold!

27
Speaking of Dancing

Matt was another dude who loved to dance. When he first came to The River he was moving around on one actual leg and one prosthetic leg (complications with his diabetes). In spite of his missing limb he could really shake a leg (sorry).

Every Sunday he stood in the back of the church and danced his heart out. When worship was done he was a sweaty mess. It was great.

Every Sunday.

Every Sunday until they had to remove his other leg (more diabetic complications).

After months of rehab, Matt was up walking on two prosthetic legs.

And dancing in the back of church.

Every Sunday.

28
Oops

We took a large group of men from The River to a men's conference. While there, we shot guns, mountain biked, road a 1,000-foot zip-line, and poured truth into the men.

Mike, a new believer, was loving it. He especially loved shooting clay pigeons. When he got back to town he downloaded some pictures onto his Facebook page that included several of him firing a shotgun at the clay pigeons.

His probation officer didn't like those pictures.

Mike got a free, all expenses paid, week-long vacation in the county jail for parole violations.

29
Bottle Rocket

We have a lot of interesting folks at The River, some of whom are not what you would call the sharpest knife in the drawer.

One Sunday morning, one such dear brother thought it would be a great idea to fire a bottle rocket off the church steps, across the street, over a police car, and into the crowded public park.

He was genuinely surprised when the officer came over, took his info, ran a background check, cuffed him, and threw him in the back of the car. Right as people were coming into church.

His probation officer didn't like his stunt at all.

Like Mike, he got a free, all expenses paid, week-long vacation in the county jail.

30
Easter Aromas

They say that smell is one of the strongest connections to memories. One whiff of something can instantly take you back to your childhood.

For me it's the smells of Easter.

The enticing smell of chocolate bunnies.

The homey scent of homemade bread to be served after church for dinner.

The succulent aroma of ham. Mmmmm.

The beautifully sweet fragrance of lilies.

Ahhhh, the smells of my childhood Easters. They almost bring tears of nostalgia to my eyes.

I have a new smell that takes me back to Easter. I call it the smell of my adult Easter. It too is a powerful memory. It too brings tears to my eyes.

We were worshiping the King of kings, celebrating the resurrection. Singing our hearts out.

While we were singing, our toilets were overflowing.

Well, not just overflowing. Barfing up the past ten years' worth of sewage is more like it. And there was no stopping the back flow. It was as if the system was saying, "Enough! Take it all back!"

On Easter! The biggest day of the church-year. More guests this day than any other. And our toilets rebelled. Talk about awful timing. It would have been one thing for the toilets to go haywire on St. Patrick's Day or Presidents Day. But Easter!? Good grief, there couldn't have been a worse day.

People were dry heaving. Guests were fleeing. Mothers were comforting their children.

The smell was horrible.

And it was Easter.

So now I have a new smell to associate with Easter.

31
Speechless

As a pastor, I often have people come to me for sympathy, support, encouragement. Most of the time I am able to offer a listening ear and a word or two by way of support and encouragement.

Most of the time.

There was one time I was speechless. Didn't know what to say. I just got up and left without a word. And asked Judy to go in my office (she's one of our pastors).

A woman had come into my office and said she needed prayer for the copious amounts of polyps on her vagina.

32
Gone

One of the awesome things about The River is that we have many folks worshiping with us who have a criminal past.

One of the not so awesome things about The River is that we have a few folks whose criminal status is not yet "past."

My oldest son, Jake, came back from my office between services one day and informed me that a gentleman was waiting in my office to talk to me. The norm is for my boys to go hang out in my office between services. On this particular day when Jake walked in there was a guy who told Jake he was waiting to talk to me.

So Jake and I walked out of the sanctuary, down the hall, up five steps, down one more hall, and into my office.

There was no one waiting to talk to me.

There also was no computer. It had been stolen.

Turns out unbeknownst to Jake he had momentarily interrupted a burglary.

We lock our office doors during service now.

33
She

One of the many beautiful things about Jesus is that he accepts us just as we are. Praise God we don't have to clean up our act before we come to him. My word, if we had to get our junk in order before we could approach God we would never be able to approach him.

Like many church plants, we've tried hard to make The River a place where anyone can come and find some warmth and welcome. I guess these stories are evidence that we've succeeded at least to some extent.

George was a man who had a pretty rough time growing up. Some abuse. A bunch of neglect. A very angry father. These wounds, among others, were contributing factors that led him to walk into the gay lifestyle.

And he walked into it with gusto. It was very apparent to anyone who laid eyes on him that he was walking in the gay lifestyle.

To everyone but Gladys that is. Gladys is our church's lone octogenarian. She was on our launch team and has been an amazing person to have around for so many reasons. Yet back in her day, men were not easily mistaken for women. Gladys simply thought George was a woman. With a beard.

This reality hit me one day when George brought some blueberries to share at church. Gladys saw the blueberries and was instantly excited. Who wouldn't be? Blueberries are awesome.

Someone seeing Gladys's excitement asked her, "What are you excited about, Gladys?" Gladys pointed at George (with his whiskery face) and said, "Look, she brought blueberries."

She? Holy smokes, what did she think? Did she just think that George was an ugly woman? I thought it was going to be an awkward moment, but Gladys was oblivious and George seemed proud.

I've never had the gumption to tell Gladys that George is a man.

34
Itchy

He was a regular at The River.

He loved animals.

One evening, as our midweek service was about to begin, someone came bursting into my office. "He's outside and is hysterical. He won't talk to anyone but you and he won't come inside."

So I went outside to see him. As I approached he yelled, "Stay back! Don't touch me!"

Hmmm...this was unusual.

I asked him what was wrong. Through many tears and wrought with fear he told me a story I will never forget.

A few weeks earlier while driving home he had accidentally run over a squirrel. Being both soft-hearted and an animal lover, he was crushed. He pulled over to see if the poor fluffy-tailed rodent was dead. As he stooped over the critter he saw that it was alive—barely.

Thinking he could bring the little fella home and nurse it

back to health, he picked it up and put it on the passenger seat in his car. By the time he got home, he realized the squirrel had died. He brought the unlucky critter inside and placed it on the kitchen counter. It was late and he was distraught, so he decided to leave the dead animal in the house until the next morning when he could hold a proper burial.

Unbeknownst to my friend, the dead animal was infested with fleas. Tons of 'em. As he slept these fleas left their furry home and made a new home in my friend's house.

Then they reproduced. Prolificly. In no time at all the house looked as if one of the plagues of Pharaoh had come to town. Fleas everywhere. Including on my friend.

He was freaked out. Didn't know what to do. He couldn't afford an exterminator. So he did nothing. And the fleas kept reproducing.

So on that night at our midweek service he came, flea-infested and scared. He was scared because he thought he would lose his home and because he didn't want to give anyone fleas.

Never in my wildest ministry dreams had I thought the church would need to care for a man infested with fleas.

This poor guy was scared to death. All he needed was several defumigators and a flea collar.

No kidding. A flea collar.

He wore one for a week until his problem was a problem no more.

35
Flu Bug

The apostle Paul says in Ephesians chapter 4 (NIV) that "Christ himself gave the apostles, the prophets, the evangelists, the pastors and teachers, to equip his people for works of service." These "equipping gifts" equip the people who are the church, the body of Christ, for ministry.

It is clear from what the Bible teaches that no one has all the gifts. That's why we need to be part of the body of believers. When we are together as a body, all the gifts are represented and unleashed.

I have a few of the equipping gifts, but not all of them. For some reason the Lord in his wisdom chose to not give me the gift of pastor/shepherd. Unfortunately folks often assume that I have the gift simply because I am employed as a pastor. Thank God—and I mean that—thank God for a great team around me that can cover the multitude of areas where I am weak.

All that to say I met a guy once who assumed and hoped to high heaven that I had the pastoral gift. And because I don't, it took every ounce of willpower I have to keep from falling over from laughing.

While we were still meeting in our first building, we needed to replace the outside doors with ones that were much more sturdy and substantial. Our volunteer building supervisor brought over a couple of guys from an industrial door company.

As they were looking at and measuring the doors, I decided to join them for a quick visit. As I walked down the aisle I noticed one of the salesmen was missing. No big deal I thought, I can visit with two as good as with three. After a brief but enjoyable chat I headed back toward my office. About half way down the aisle, the other salesman appeared out of nowhere.

To say he looked sheepish would be a gross (and I mean gross, as you will soon find out) understatement. Picture a puppy that got caught chewing on slippers and knew he was in trouble. That was this guy.

He looked up at me with embarrassment and shame emanating from his eyes, begging me to be pastoral without saying a word.

"Uh…pastor, I had an accident."

Having been a pastor for a number of years by this time, I knew when and how to switch into kind mode. "I'm sorry. What kind of accident?" I asked in a kind and caring voice. Mother Teresa would have been proud of me.

"Well, uh, I, uh… you see, I've had the flu and I, well, I… I didn't make it to your bathroom."

At this point my make-Mother-Teresa-proud-voice faded into nothingness. I said, "Huh?" (Profound, I know). I could tell my lack of understanding made this dude even more uncomfortable.

"I, uh, I didn't make it to your bathroom."

I was still confused.

"I'm sorry. I'm not sure what you're saying."

"I pooped on your floor."

I thought he was joking, so I started to laugh. I said, "Really? Well, that stinks, ha, ha, ha." I thought he would chuckle at my quick, albeit sophomoric, wit.

Instead he turned a deeper shade of red.

"I'm really sorry. I've been fighting this flu bug, and just couldn't make it."

"Oh."

That's about as pastoral as I could get. Sorry, Mother Teresa.

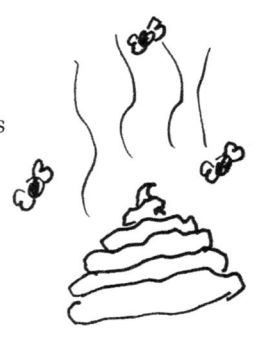

"I'm really embarrassed and don't want my partner or your building supervisor to know. Can I come back in a couple hours to clean it up?"

"Uh, you want to leave, let your poop sit on the floor for a couple hours, then come back and clean it up?"

"Yes," he mumbled.

"Well, uh, I guess so."

He finished his business—with the doors, that is—left, dropped off his partner, came back with bucket and supplies in tow, cleaned, and left. Never saw him again.

36
Reap What You Sow

Throughout Scripture the principle of reaping what you sow is evident. It's a true thing.

Trust me. I've learned the hard way.

One hobby I've enjoyed over the years is scaring people. I've had the pleasure of engaging in this hobby often at The River.

Unbeknownst to me the staff decided enough was enough.

Arriving back at the church late one night after a meeting, Wil invited me into his office to talk about something "really important." While we were having our important meeting Fraaz (who had gone to my house earlier in the day and snagged the extra key to my car) snuck into the back seat of my Honda Element.

After our meeting, which seemed a lot less important to me than it did to Wil, we made our way out to our vehicles. As I climbed into the driver's seat I smelled something stinky.

"Phew," I said out loud. I thought it was stinky gym clothes. In actuality it was Fraaz's fart, which almost betrayed the surprise he had in store for me.

I started my car, shifted into reverse, and looked in the rearview mirror. The moment I looked in the mirror Fraaz sprang up from nowhere, yelling at the top of his lungs, and grabbed my shoulders.

I about messed my drawers right there. For a moment I had strong empathy for the door salesman in the last story.

I've since curtailed my engagement in this hobby.

37
Drool

Fraaz and I were taking Barkly for a walk one afternoon. In my back pocket I had Barkly's slobber hanky. As mentioned before, Barkly is the Newfoundland dog on staff at The River as a greeter. What I didn't mention before is that he drools like a champ.

If there was a competition for drooling Barkly would win hands down. If I'm not handy with the hanky, massive, ten-inch-long gobs of goobery dog spit will appear at the corners of Barkly's mouth, hanging down like nasty, slobbery stalactites.

On this particular walk I had just bent down to wipe Barkly's mouth. As I stood, a gentleman came over to pet him. As the man bent over to pet Barkly, he drooled. The man, not the dog. A big, long string of man spit came pouring out of his mouth and hit the sidewalk right in front of my dog.

I'm not kidding. You can ask Fraaz. The man drooled. Almost as good as Barkly.

I decided not to offer him the hanky.

38
Dance

The Bible tells us that King David stripped down to his undergarments and danced before the Lord when the Ark of the Covenant was brought into Jerusalem.

We love freedom in worship at The River. But we do have one rule. Keep your clothes on. We don't want folks stripping down to their undergarments.

It's not uncommon to see people dancing in the aisle during our worship times.

One day, Steve was taking the liberty to exhibit freedom in worship.

At first I thought it was awesome to see a dude dance unbridled and undignified before the Lord.

As he jumped up on the steps going up toward the stage and started doing the Madonna Vogue dance where he would use a sideways peace sign with alternating hands to cover his eyes, I began to wonder if one could take this freedom in worship thing to far.

Next thing I knew he was casting an imaginary fishing pole toward Judy, our prayer pastor. He began to "reel" her in as he moved closer and closer to her.

When he started to dirty dance with our non-participating prayer pastor, it was time to intervene.

I gently but firmly pulled him aside and sat him down. That's when the smell hit me. He reeked of alcohol and marijuana. I almost got high smelling the guy.

We still only have one rule in worship. Remembering this story makes me wonder if we ought to have two.

1. Keep your clothes on. 2. No dirty dancing in worship.

39
Object Lesson Gone Bad

Like most preachers these days we work hard at making it hard for the hearers of the Word to zone out and check out during the teaching.

While Fraaz (our worship pastor) was preparing to preach (he does this once in a while, handing his worship-leading duties to another) he thought long and hard how he might both engage the congregation and drive the point home. He came up with a seemingly brilliant idea.

He was preaching on worship and making the point that worship was much more than music. "Worship encompasses all of life" was the message he wanted to get across.

Earlier in the week, to help make this point, he had purchased a couple of cheap guitars at a local pawn shop.

At the climatic point in his message he picked up a guitar. Folks didn't know it was not his good guitar but rather the cheap pawn-shop one. As he made the point that worship is more than music, he smashed his guitar on the stage in a way that would make any '80s metal band proud.

The crowd gasped.

Well done, Fraaz. Point made.

People were stunned.

Fraaz was more stunned.

As he smashed the guitar a sharp shard of wood shot back into his face, nailing him right in the forehead.

Opening a gash.

That bled. Right down between his eyebrows and over his nose.

The crowd gasped again.

Well done, Fraaz.

40
Stupid

We believe that God will speak to us today. Certainly through the Word, but also through his Spirit to an individual. (Of course the word from the Lord cannot contradict Scripture.)

There are times when I "hear" the still, small voice in my heart with a word for the people. Most of the time, when I share the word with the folks they are blessed and God is glorified.

Most of the time.

There was a time when we were a multi-site church. Since then we've sent one site in the direction of a new church plant and the other we've pulled back into our larger site.

I had just made my way over to the Lake Street site after preaching at our downtown location. I was always cutting it close, as the times were stacked one right after the other. We had a team of people who opened the doors and got everything ready for the day's worship service. All I had to do was show up and preach.

On this particular Sunday I pulled into the parking lot to see a crowd of folks standing outside the door.

I thought: What the heck!? The stinkin' doors are still locked! Who dropped the dang ball on this one?

I parked, got out, and unlocked the church doors. I went inside with the bulk of the people. The sanctuary was a mess. The worship team wasn't even close to being ready.

What the heck is going on here? Where is the site pastor? Where is the launch team? Whose incompetence is this!? These thoughts screamed through my head.

And then I heard what I thought was the voice of the Lord inside my head. And let me tell you, me and the Lord were going to stick it to the people that day!

Eventually the service began—incredibly late, I might add. After a song or two I couldn't contain the word that I had so I waved off the worship team and stood up to give the word.

Here is a synopsis of what I said that day;

"If you are a guest I am sorry that you are here today. The people of this site do not care enough about you to be prepared. If you are a visitor you are free to leave. I have some words for the folks who call this their home.

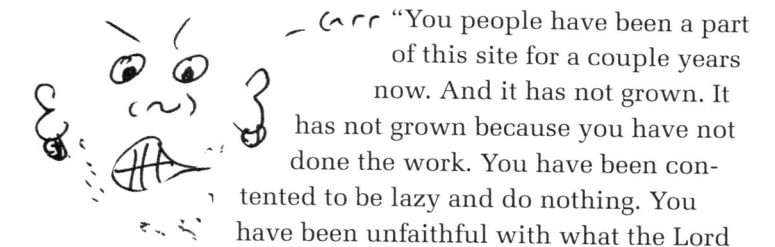

"You people have been a part of this site for a couple years now. And it has not grown. It has not grown because you have not done the work. You have been contented to be lazy and do nothing. You have been unfaithful with what the Lord has given you. This site is a mess and you are responsible.

"I am tired of trying to fix your problem. The mess is yours to fix. So you fix it. It is up to you. I'm leaving."

With that, a mere ten minutes into the service I left. Just walked out and left the folks to figure it out on their own.

I went home and actually felt pretty good about my presentation.

Until our site pastor called.

Bottom line: he said what I did was stupid.

He was right.

As soon as he spoke I realized I had been in error. Major error.

I had "misheard." The stress of life (a buddy just diagnosed with cancer, a week-long meeting an hour away I was driving back and forth to, and the disappointment with the site) crippled my spiritual ears. What I thought I heard from the Lord was just my poor attitude.

Stupid.

The next week we started the service at that site with me apologizing, repenting, and asking for forgiveness for my hurtful stupidity.

The folks were very gracious as they gathered around me and prayed for me.

Thank God for grace.

41
More Stupid

Sally used to work at The River as our administrative assistant. To say that our personalities were like cats and dogs would be an understatement.

For what seemed like the hundredth time we had some issue arise between us. I was angry. I had had enough. So I was going to go and tell her I was tired of it all.

Now, keep in mind that the Bible does say to address problems you have with people with the person you have the problem with. This was the verse that was resonating in my head.

Well the Bible also says to not sin in your anger.

Oops, I had overlooked that one at the moment.

As I was walking down the hall to confront her, Fraaz stepped in front of me, put his hand on my chest and said, "Not now. Go cool down."

Being the reasonable sort, always open to wise counsel, I ignored him, pulled my best wax-off move (see the original Karate Kid movie if that confuses you), went down to her office, and commenced giving her a piece of my mind.

Boy, did it feel good.

For about a minute.

As soon as I sat down in my office, the conviction of the Spirit was all over me.

I got back up and sheepishly made the same walk down the same hall and apologized.

To be honest, I don't think that relationship ever recovered.

42
Weird Lunch

One day Dori (our family pastor) and Anna (our communications director and one of our worship leaders) were meeting in the park for lunch.

They were interrupted.

By a woman who was highly attracted to Anna and tried to pick her up for a date.

That's a weird lunch.

43
Clean

When Sue worked for us the church had never been cleaner. She was awesome at keeping the place spotless. In fact it probably hasn't been as clean since she got fired.

She really loved to clean. The problem was that she and her stepson (unbeknownst to us) were addicted to crack. While she was cleaning he would break into our Joy Boxes (place where folks drop off their tithes and offerings) and help himself to support his and Sue's drug habits.

We realized we had a problem one day when we found a month's worth of checks crumpled up behind a cabinet.

I had thought our people were just being stingy. Turns out we had a thief on our hands.

Sue lost her job.

The church hasn't been as clean since.

44
Second Chance

Praise the Lord, he is a God of second chances.

My goodness, each and every one of us has needed grace and a second chance time after time. I can't even imagine what life would be like if second chances were not part of it.

With that in mind, we gave Sue another shot and rehired her as our janitor (after she had spent extensive time in rehab).

Things were going along well.

For about a year.

Then one Friday morning her issues were getting the best of her. After a verbal tirade that would have made a sailor blush, she threw her keys at Wil and said, "F%#@ you! I quit!"

Wil immediately accepted her resignation.

Sunday morning rolls around, and Sue shows up to do her work as if nothing is wrong.

Wil graciously reminded her of her resigning two days earlier and reminded her that she no longer was employed with us.

And that was that.

45
Anger Issues

And that was that. Or so we thought.

Sue left the building and went and got her husband, Simon.

Simon has anger issues.

He commenced to storm into the building, cornered Wil, proved that his wife was actually a novice when it comes to swearing, and threatened very loudly to kick Wil's "M%$#*& F*&%#$% A&@." All this just moments before the service was about to begin.

Simon not only has anger issues, he's big. Easily tips the scales at 260.

The Word tells us that we do not live with a spirit of fear or timidity but rather a spirit of power.

Wil, walking in the Spirit with the power of the Spirit,

stood up to Simon, talked him off the ledge, and had him crying for forgiveness in a matter of moments.

That's awesome.

46
Breakfast in Bed

One of the "least of these" was sleeping on our step one Sunday morning.

When I arrived one of our worship team members had placed a blanket over her, set some breakfast next to her along with a thermos of coffee so that when she awoke she could have breakfast in bed.

When she did awaken she was warmly greeted and ushered into the church.

She became a part of the family that day.

47
Confused

She was confused as to why we wouldn't let her work with kids after her background check.

After her arrest for arson, child abuse, and fraud and subsequent jail time, she found some clarity.

48
Crack House

Jesus tells the story of the shepherd who leaves the ninety-nine sheep of his flock to go find the one lost sheep.

Keith took that story literally.

One of his small-group members had relapsed into her addiction. Long before the relapse, her small group had vowed to be there for her when she needed them.

The word on the street was that she was back hanging out at the old crack house.

Keith grabbed another dude from the group, drove to the crack house, and asked her to leave the house with him.

She refused.

Keith and the other guy reminded her of their promise to her.

He picked her up over his shoulder and carried her out of the house.

She was screaming.

The crack dealer was confused.

Keith was acting like Jesus.

49
Dancing with Both Legs

Earlier I told the story of Matt, who had two prothestic legs and loved to dance during worship.

It had been a while since we had seen him. He wasn't returning phone calls. He didn't answer the door when the men from his small group stopped by to check on him.

Turns out he had died, alone in his trailer, as a result of complications from his diabetes.

That one hit us hard.

Still does.

It does ease the pain a bit knowing he is now dancing in heaven.

On two legs.

50
Another Matt Story

He was unbridled in his joy each Sunday.

He really, really, really loved coming to church, hanging out with his family, and worshiping.

During the teaching, folks regularly comment back and forth with me while I'm teaching.

I like that a lot. Most of the time the comments are well placed, appropriate, and not at all a distraction.

Most of the time.

One day I was teaching on the topic of "fishing for people."

I had just finished saying the word "fish," and it was dead quiet in the building.

It was then that Matt responded to an inner urge and yelled at the top of his lungs, "Fish on!"

It was so loud and ill-timed it scared everyone.

From my vantage point from the front it was kinda funny to see everybody jump out of their skin.

Matt instantly knew his timing was off and ducked down onto the floor to hide.

So there we were with folks so startled many had to change their drawers and another guy lying on the floor in the fetal position trying to hide.

Again, my seminary education hadn't prepared me for such a time.

So I just laughed.

Loudly.

51
Strike Two (Or Maybe Three)

Remember the story of our janitor, Sue?

We replaced her with a guy named Ted. He was down on his luck, and we thought we would help him out by hiring him to do maintenance and janitorial work.

We had to fire him after he was caught stealing money from the church and using the church computers to feed his porn habit.

52
(Un)Lucky

If ever there was a misnomer it was the name of this dog, Lucky.

Lucky belonged to one of our members who wrestled with mental illness.

Unfortunately for both Lucky and his owner, mental illness was winning.

Lucky's owner had been checked into the hospital for a while when he called Wil and asked him to go check on Lucky.

Wil did.

When he opened the door to the apartment, Wil gagged and just about threw up. Poor Lucky had been left for weeks. There were dog feces everywhere. It became clear that after he had eaten all the food he could reach Lucky was surviving (barely) by eating his own poop.

As a church we went into action and contacted the SPCA.

Lucky eventually found a new home.

When Lucky's now former owner got out, he sued Wil for stealing his dog.

53
A Great Idea

Right across the street from our building is this awesome park. It is smack dab in the center of Kalamazoo and has this awesome band shell.

We thought it would be a great idea to have an outdoor service there.

We checked with the city and got their approval.

Instead of two services, that day we had one large, loud, outdoor worship fest.

It was incredible.

Or I should say it was incredible until representatives from the other churches around the park began to storm out angrily and assault our sound technician.

One guy from the church across from us came out looking for someone to slaughter. I found out he was one of their elders, and serves as a school administrator (i.e. is used to being in a position of authority). He stands 6 feet 10 inches tall and weighs around 175.

I'm not kidding when I say it looked like Ichabod Crane was coming to kill somebody.

Another pastor stood on his doorstep and scowled. After his service was over he came and asked Fraaz, "Could you hear our music?"

Fraaz innocently answered, "No."

The other pastor continued, his words dripping with sarcasm, "Well, we couldn't either, thanks to you." He then marched away.

I spent the next week making the rounds apologizing for our great idea.

54
Spotter

I've told you the story of a guy named Walt who routinely fell asleep during the service.

He wasn't (isn't) the only one.

John falls asleep regularly too.

And he snores.

I told you Walt snored loudly. Well, compared to John, Walt's snores sound like a soothing breeze.

John snores so loudly and regularly that we have a person sit next to him (unbeknownst to John) to act as a spotter.

When John snores our spotter gently and expertly nudges him until he wakes up and stops snoring.

55
What the Heck Was That?!

The River is a part of the Reformed Church in America (RCA), a great, wonderful, and historic denomination that wonderfully accentuates God's grace. The RCA has a long tradition of solid, biblical teaching.

Yet if there is one thing that has been missing in the RCA, it is a balanced embrace of the Holy Spirit. In general we Reformed folk have been very comfortable with the Father and the Son, but have been a bit nervous around the Spirit.

So to rectify that, many of us from The River drove out to Pennsylvania to attend a charismatic conference, hoping to shore up our understanding and experience of and with the Holy Spirit.

Needless to say, we were blown away. We encountered the Spirit in many amazing ways and a few crazy ones.

As was the case for many of us, Barry was a bit skeptical about the things he was seeing. Many of us had some pretty cool Spirit encounters, while Barry hadn't encountered anything but some weirdness.

With those two things in mind (skepticism and no encounter) Barry said at dinner one night, "I want to experience the Spirit so powerfully that there is no doubt it is of God!"

He had no idea what he was asking.

Later that night, during the ministry time, people were experiencing powerful and strange (at least strange to a bunch of RCA folks) things. Barry went storming up front to have one of the ministry team members pray for him.

A young woman, no older than 25, turned to pray for him. When she lifted her hand to pray, Barry went flying backward.

Literally!

It was as if an invisible linebacker had nailed him. He must've flown ten feet backward and landed hard on his back.

And yet he wasn't hurt at all. In fact the opposite was true. He felt euphoric. No pain. Those who saw it happen were sure he was going to be in a boat-load of pain. But there was none.

For the next 45 minutes or so he couldn't move. He simply lay there under the soft hand of the Spirit and felt overwhelmed with love.

When Barry got up, we asked him, "What the heck was that?"

He said, "An experience that was no doubt from God."

He'd gotten exactly what he'd asked for.

56
Speechless...Again

I almost didn't include this story for reasons that will soon be apparent. Yet a couple of folks from The River encouraged me to include it for the sake of giving an authentic picture. So here I go. Forgive me for listening to those two.

We were at a church potluck when she came up to me and said, "I had a dream about you last night."

"Uh oh," I said, alarm bells going off in my head.

She was a 60ish-year-old woman who up until this point had shown herself to have good self-awareness and a decent level of social grace.

At the potluck she forgot about such things.

"Yeah, in my dream you and I were walking up to the front door of your house."

In my head I was thinking, "OK, so far this is all right."

"And you were naked."

What? I screamed inside my head.

"When we opened the door Kristy [my wife] was coming down the stairs wearing a wedding gown."

Whew, I thought. The awkward moment is behind us.

I thought wrong.

"And you were wringing out your penis like a wash cloth."

That, my friends, is a direct quote.

I can honestly say I never have been so embarrassed in my whole life.

And confused. Like a wash cloth?! How is that even possible?

I set my plate down, got up, left the building, and drove home.

57
Hypomania

Hypomania is a condition in which neural transmitters are slow-firing. Someone with hypomania has a slow-firing "appropriateness" filter. When you or I think about saying or doing something inappropriate, our screening system says, "I shouldn't actually say (or do) that."

Someone with hypomania has no such screening system (for example, the woman in the previous story).

We discovered Wil has hypomania. Fortunately for all involved, once we sent him to a therapist he overcame this hurdle.

You might ask, "How did you know he had it, and why did you send him to a therapist?"

Let me tell you.

We were at a large denominational gathering. You know the type. Hundreds of people. Suits, ties. Formal.

Our regional governing body had brought in a nationally renowned speaker, seated us at circular tables in groups of six, and set us up for some gripping dialogue.

I happened to be assigned to lead the discussion at my table.

The speaker had just finished and handed it over to us facilitators to commence the dialogue.

The discussion at my table was deep and rich.

Then things went horribly awry.

I was making a point, when everyone at my table stopped looking at me and instead looked immediately to my left. I could see several people from other tables looking to my left as well.

So I followed the crowd and looked to my left.

Wil was sitting there with his pants hiked up above his belly (think Tweedle Dee) and his shirt pulled up over his face with his nipples staring at anyone and everyone unfortunate enough to be looking in his direction.

I, along with everyone else, was stunned.

The only thing going through my head was, What the h#@* is he doing?!

Turns out he was having a hypomania moment.

Thank God for therapists.

58
More Puppy Love

Deb was down and out the first time she ever came to The River. So much so that she later told me she was scared to death to come to church. The only reason she came was because the local gospel mission expected their residents to go to church.

So she came to The River.

And met Barkly.

You'll remember he is my dog who serves at church each week as a greeter. He's a Newfoundland and weighs around 165 pounds.

Deb and Barkly fell in love instantly.

Each week she would come around the corner, sit on the ground, and have a little puppy love-fest with Barkly.

He absolutely loved it. Which is why he is a greeter.

She loved it too.

She loved Barkly so much that she signed up for the

Thursday morning women's Bible study my wife was teaching at our house, in large part so she could see Barkly.

I often take Barkly with me when I leave the house, so Deb was often mad at me for not leaving Barkly at home for her to see on Bible study days.

One Thursday morning I was out of town at a conference. About twenty minutes after Bible study had ended, Kristy looked out the window. There were Deb and Barkly. He was standing up on his back legs, looking her in the eye.

No joke. They were hugging.

Kristy told me that at that moment Deb looked filled with peace and joy.

Deb died a week later.

Her parents flew up from Florida for the funeral. Someone else on staff had handled all the logistics with the family. All I was responsible for was to show up at the funeral home and preach at the funeral.

I walked in and went straight to Deb's parents to offer my condolences. Her mother didn't let me finish before she asked, "Where is Barkly?"

I told her he was taking a nap out in my car.

"You have to go get him and bring him in. Every week I talked to Deb on the phone she told me about Barkly. He needs to be in here as a part of this service."

I gently tried to protest. It was a funeral after all. Dogs just aren't allowed.

The funeral director also protested.

Mom would hear none of it.

So on that day, Barkly did his first funeral.

He walked up front with me when it was time to teach.

The reaction from the crowd was amazing. It was as if a healing wind blew through the place when this big, furry hound came in.

He sat down.

I taught.

Joy filled the room. At a funeral.

Amazing.

59
Farewell

Jessica and Jonathon were a part of our family at The River for years. They lived at the mission. They were very kind and filled with love.

They had to move to Ohio.

One Sunday, right in the middle of my teaching, Jessica came into the building, walked down the middle of the aisle, stood in front of me, interrupted the sermon, and said, "I'm moving tomorrow and wanted to tell you good bye. Good bye, Rob. Where's Kristy so I can tell her bye, too?"

I told her Kristy was serving in the nursery.

I said, "Good bye."

I resumed preaching.

60
Dropping Acid

Before service one day a bunch of us were standing outside greeting folks and chatting away.

Out of nowhere this dude approaches one of the guys getting ready to go into church and throws a whole jar of acid on his face!

One man went down.

Another ran away.

The police and an ambulance came.

And I had to go preach.

61
Flu Bug Hits Again

Each Sunday we have a pancake breakfast before the first service. Our goal is to build community across demographic lines. Usually it is a pretty cool, uneventful gathering.

Usually.

Remember the story about the salesman who had a bout with the flu on our bathroom floor?

Well, it happened again.

At pancake breakfast.

All over the floor.

The smell of sausage is a wonderful complement to pancakes.

This smell wasn't.

A lot of leftover pancakes that day.

62
Pancake Batter and Assault

Like I said, our pancake breakfasts are usually uneventful.

Usually.

One morning, right in the middle of our fellowship hall, George and Ralph decided to continue an argument they had been having earlier.

Our security team ushered them outside, where George proceeded to beat the tar out of Ralph.

63
Batter Up

One Sunday morning, my oldest son, Jake, Barkly, Wil, and I were outside greeting people.

Tom came around the corner brandishing an aluminum baseball bat, swearing up a storm, telling the world how he is going to "f@#* up" so and so, who is inside the church getting coffee.

He saw us, turned toward the park across the street, and kept mumbling to himself. He stood glaring at the front door of the church.

Honest to goodness, Jake looked at him, looked at me, shrugged his shoulders, and went back to business. This was nothing out of the ordinary for him.

When I asked him about his nonchalance, he said, "Dad, I hear the 'F word' more at church than I do anywhere else."

Eventually the dude left. No one got battered.

64
Speaking of Assault and Battery

I came around the corner from our little parking lot, and there was Danny.

Danny was mad.

Very mad.

At me.

Danny began to tell me and everyone within a ten-mile radius how he was going to beat me up. He began to question my lineage with regard to my mother, my father, and all my ancestors. He berated me for my overt lack of intelligence.

Amazingly he was able to do this while weaving in the "F word" nearly every other word.

I tried to ignore him and walked right past him. I went inside into my office and sat down.

Danny followed me in. He was ballistic. He was looming over me as I sat in my chair and continued to verbally assault me.

He was clearly unstable. (Yes, I do have the gift of discernment.) I began to think that this dude might be a physical threat not only to me but to anybody in the building.

For the first and only time in my life I said to myself, I'm gonna have to kick a parishioner's butt.

No joke. I thought I was going to have to disable him.

I stood up ready to punch him. As I stood up Wil and Fraaz walked in my office.

I failed to mention that Danny is a whopping 5' 9". I stand 6' 5", Fraaz is 6' 3", and Wil is 6' 6". Danny couldn't have weighed more than 180 pounds, while each of us weighs over 200.

As soon as I stood up ready to punch him and the fellas walked in, Danny went as meek as a mouse. Imagine that.

We ushered him outside, shut the door, and turned to go about our business.

Danny instantly went nuts the moment we went back inside. He began throwing rocks at our windows and yelling threats at the top of his lungs.

We called the police.

Four policemen came.

Danny settled down.

For a minute.

The police wouldn't let me leave through the front door, since I was the source of Danny's agitation. I had to sneak out the back door.

At one point Danny got belligerent with the policemen and began to walk away, throwing threatening words over his shoulder.

One of the policemen said, "Wrong move, son," and tackled Danny from behind with form that would have made an NFL scout proud.

As soon as the one cop had him down, two more jumped on top, effectively pinning Danny underneath three policemen.

The fourth policeman got the cuffs out and read Danny his rights.

Danny got a free ride to jail.

All in all he might have been better off had he and I simply duked it out.

65
Inner Thespian

Just between you and me, I'll admit that there is a part of me that likes to act. Not saying I'm a secret drama king, but maybe a secret drama prince.

Sometimes my inner thespian breaks out while I'm preaching. Usually it's simply expressed as a flair for the dramatic during a story or the dramatic lowering of my voice to make a point.

But one time I thought it would be a good idea to do a first-person sermon.

I got this sweet robe-outfit thing, just like they would've worn in Bible times.

I spent hours memorizing lines from Genesis and the account of Abraham.

I even grew a beard.

For weeks I laid awake at night dreaming of how powerful and moving this would be for the congregation.

There would be weeping.

There would be repentance.

And of course, there would be a little affirmation of what a good actor I was.

The Sunday eventually arrived, and I donned both my outfit and my game face. I was serious. Something was going to happen this day!

I opened the side door for my dramatic entrance.

I stoically and Abraham-ically walked onto the stage.

And the people…and the people…

Laughed.

Uncontrollably.

For a long time.

This was not what I was going for.

Drama, not humor, was my intent.

Yet the people only saw humor.

Longest time I ever spent preaching. Seemed like hours—it was only minutes.

I went home that day and threw the stupid robe away.

66
Greater Is He

The sound coming from our prayer room was like something out of *The Exorcist*.

That's because it was the beginning of an exorcism.

Our prayer pastor at the time, Cheri, had taken a woman who had come in off the streets into the prayer room to pray over her. All hell broke loose.

Literally.

Wil, Fraaz, and I joined Cheri for what would be a first exorcism for all of us.

It was crazy.

The woman was thrashing around on the floor, frothing at the mouth, laughing at us with a deep and guttural voice.

And the room stunk like a wet animal.

Wil, Cheri, and I began to pray while Fraaz ran to get his guitar.

When he returned he began to worship.

She began to hawk lugies and spit at him.

Like some kind of worship ninja, Fraaz dodged spit and mucus while playing his guitar and did not miss a note. Not one lick of spit landed on him.

Astounding.

At one point the woman jumped up and put both hands around my neck as if to choke me. As soon as she touched me she fell back to the ground.

We looked at each other knowingly. He that is in us is greater than he that is in the world.

Or in this case, he that is in Cheri, Wil, Fraaz, and I is

greater than he who was in this woman.

Not long after she tried to strangle me, her demeanor changed drastically. It was as if she had awoken from a nap. She was not the same writhing, foul-mouthed woman she had been a short time before. The wet-animal smell even left the room.

The woman became a regular part of The River until she moved out of town.

He that is in you is greater than he that is in the world.

* * * * *

Words are tricky. With the simple inflection of the voice the same word can either be hurtful or helpful.

When I named this book *Rascals* I realized there was a risk that the intended inflection might be missed. So let me make it clear.

I picture Abba holding each person whose story is in this book on his mighty and safe lap while playfully giving them a noogie on the top of their head. All the while lovingly saying, "You little rascal."

Rascal. A term of love, affection, and endearment.

Rascal defines us well.

Loved by the Father describes us even better.